This coloring book b

This coloring book belongs to:

Sugar Skulls Coloring Book For Kids © 2019 by Frijolitos Coloring Books
All rights reserved. No part of this book may be used or reproduced in any manner whatsoever without written permission except in the case of brief quotations embodied in critical articles and reviews.
First Edition: 2019

Made in the USA
Las Vegas, NV
08 March 2024

86899367R00031